NORTH AMERICAN INDIAN LIFE

BY

JOHN D. CLARE

Who were the North American Indians?

The American Indians spoke many different languages. When the Europeans arrived, as many as 2,200 existed. In addition, they developed a common sign language that allowed them to communicate effectively with other tribes.

TO DO, TO MAKE

Place your hands together with the fingertips of your right hand touching the palm of your left. Lift both hands and shake your wrists.

TEPEE

Hold knuckles lightly together, and touch the tips of your index fingers together to make the shape of a tepee.

THE CAVALRY ARE COMING

In the 16th century, settlers from Europe began to come to North America. In the 19th century, they began to head west. Within 50 years, Europeans had taken much of the American Indians' land and destroyed their way of life. They believed that it had been their 'manifest destiny' to do so.

Since the 19th century, people have been fascinated by North American Indians. They have been portrayed in books, travelling shows and, more recently, in films and television programmes. Yet for all that, they are still misunderstood. Even the name 'Indians' is misleading. Christopher Columbus called the inhabitants of the New World 'Indians' because he mistakenly thought he had sailed to India. One problem is that much of what we know about the North American Indians was set down by white men. Some wrote to justify the slaughter and mistreatment of the native population. Another problem is that the American Indians lived and thought in a way that is alien to most of us today.

THANKSGIVING

In 1622, the Mayflower Pilgrims, helped by the Wampanoag Indians who lived nearby, managed to bring in a good harvest. Half the Pilgrims had died in the winter of 1621, so in 1622, they joined in the Indians' annual 'Thanksgiving' ceremony. The custom continued, and in 1863, Abraham Lincoln declared Thanksgiving a national holiday. In Plymouth, Massachusetts, there is a bronze statue of the Wampanoag chief, Massasoit. The inscription on the figure reads: *'Protector and Preserver of the Pilgrims'.*

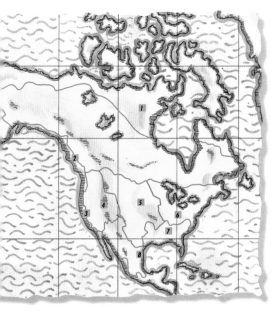

NORTH AMERICAN INDIAN SETTLEMENTS

1 ARCTIC *Inuit.*

2 PACIFIC NORTHWEST *Chilkat, Coos, Kwakiutl, Tlingit, Tsimshian.*

3 CALIFORNIA *Yokut.*

4 ROCKY MOUNTAINS *Shoshoni.*

5 GREAT PLAINS *Arapaho, Blackfeet, Cheyenne, Crow, Mandan, Sioux.*

6 NORTHEAST *Algonquian, Chippewa, Huron, Midewiwin, Mohawk, Sauk.*

7 SOUTHEAST *Cherokee, Choctaw, Creek.*

8 SOUTHWEST *Apache, Hopi, Navajo, Paiute, Pima, Pueblo, Zuni.*

THE CANYON OF THE DEAD

The Canyon de Chelly illustrates both the beauty and the history of the American West – part of the Canyon is called 'Canyon del Muerto' (Spanish for 'Canyon of the Dead'). This is because of a series of bloody military encounters that occured there, and also because of the 'mummy caves' in the region which hold human remains. The whole area is steeped in American Indian mythology. Spider Rock, a huge pillar of rock in the Canyon more than 250 metres (850 ft) high, is the home of Spider Woman in Navajo legends (see page 18). Navajo Indians still live in the Canyon de Chelly today.

PRE-COLUMBIAN CUP

DNA and language studies suggest that all American Indians are descended from a few families who crossed the Bering Strait in the late Ice Age. By 1492, when Columbus 'discovered' America, they were living all over the continent. One particularly advanced group – the Anasazi – lived in what is now the Arizona desert. At their height, the Anasazi numbered about 5,000 people, and they accumulated huge mounds of broken pottery, which included cups like the one shown left.

HORSE RIDER

Hold your left hand slightly downwards, straight out in the 'cuts paper' shape. Hold the fingers of your right hand in the 'scissors' shape, and slide onto the index finger of the left hand, as a rider would sit on a horse.

TRADE OR EXCHANGE

Make a fist with both hands, and touch the finger knuckles together. Raise both index fingers to make a 'steeple'.

YOU

Hold your hand in a fist and point your index finger towards the person you are referring to.

SETTLEMENT OR TOWN

A settlement is a group of people living together, so hold hands slightly downwards and interlock your fingers at the ends. Point your two thumbs towards each other.

Wealth & Government

owadays, 'the American Dream' is to work hard and become wealthy, important and famous. Many American Indians had a completely different attitude. They traded extensively, and some of them became very rich. But they refused to accumulate wealth, and acquired it mainly to give it away in shows of generosity. They thought the white man's habit of accumulating food and possessions was greedy and they suspected that someone who stored up wealth was a witch! Similarly, American Indians developed a way of government that was completely different to that found in European societies. Some Europeans even claimed that they had no government at all, but others conceded that – though they were impossible for the white man to understand – American Indian ways seemed to work quite well for the American Indians.

TOTEM POLE

The totem poles of the northwestern Indian tribes were symbols of a family's social position and importance. This involved not only their lineage (family), but also their clan (a group of families) and their moiety (a wide grouping of clans, linked by a common mythical ancestor). This totem pole shows a thunderbird ancestor, with other carvings symbolizing the owner's family, marriage alliances and other important events.

TRIBAL CHIEFS

European governments needed punishments to force their subjects to obey. American Indians co-operated voluntarily. Individuals were allowed to disagree and go their own way – even if the elders of the tribe recommended war, it was up to each warrior to decide whether to fight or not. There were few punishments – the worst punishment for an American Indian was to be banished (asked to leave the tribe).

POTLATCH CEREMONY

This photograph shows three head men of the Chilkat tribe of the northwest at a social event called a *potlatch*. The chiefs of the northwest coast held potlatches to demonstrate their wealth. It was obligatory to give the guests great feasts, and to load them with gifts. The most important aspect of a potlatch, however, was that guests were then obliged to hold a return potlatch, at which they had to give back twice as many presents as they had received. A potlatch, therefore, was a form of 'fighting with wealth', as chiefs tried to bankrupt their rivals.

A MANDAN CHIEF

This painting shows Four Bears, the last chief of the Mandan Indians of the Great Plains. European visitors were amazed at how little power the chiefs had. An American Indian chief could not strike the youngest warrior (even in the middle of a battle) and, at home, the only people who obeyed him were his own family. He relied on the 'influence' that he had gained by his feats in battle. The feathers in Four Bears' war bonnet showed that he was a great warrior, and the knife in his headdress recalled a battle with a Cheyenne chief.

POLE PERFECTION

The great age of totem poles came after 1850, when the American Indian carvers obtained European steel knives and chisels. Families and villages competed to commission the largest and most ornate poles – some stood 30 metres (90 ft) high. The figure on top of the totem pole on the right is a guardian spirit. On top of its hat are potlatch rings, showing that the owner of the house has held a number of successful potlatches.

Life for Ordinary Indians

When he first saw the American Indians in 1859, the prejudiced American journalist Horace Greeley decided that they belonged *'to the lowest ages of human existence – squalid and conceited, proud and worthless, lazy and lousy, they strut out their miserable existence, and at last give the world relief by dying out of it'*. Conversely, present-day writers tend to depict American Indian life in an over-romanticized way. In truth, life for 'ordinary' American Indians varied greatly, but most Europeans of the era would have found the Native American lifestyle uncomfortable and dangerous.

EXPOSURE

Life on the Great Plains was particularly hard, as the weather-beaten face of this old Plains Indian woman shows. One result of this was a custom known as 'exposure' – sometimes, when the tribe moved on to another camp, they would leave an old person behind to starve. Old people realized that moving on might be the difference between life and death for the rest of the tribe, and often did not want to travel with their families. When George Catlin spoke to one such old man, he was told: *'I am a burden to my children and I wish to die'.*

CHOCTAW INDIAN ENCAMPMENT

Most American Indian tribes were either nomadic or semi-nomadic as in many parts of North America the weather was too unreliable to rely on farming. Many tribes spent most of the year living off the environment as hunter-gatherers. In the winter, the Choctaw Indians of the southeast prepared the fields and planted crops such as maize, sunflowers and sweet potatoes. In the summer, they left to go fishing and to gather fruits and berries. During this time they lived in rough, temporary wooden shelters.

STORY-TELLING

When the Europeans arrived in America in 1492, the American Indians had no written language. Much of their leisure time was spent listening to stories. This meant the myths and customs of the tribe were passed down from one generation to the next. Sometimes, a story-teller unable to walk would be carried by the young men from one village to the next, so eager were the American Indians to hear the traditional stories. In this way, an aged or disabled person could play a valuable role within society.

BEAR HUNT

American Indian bows and arrows were not powerful enough to bring down a bear, so the hunters had to kill the bear at close range. They had to go in close, then slip round under its paws and stab it in the side. Bear hunting, therefore, was very dangerous! Before they attacked the bear, American Indian hunters often prayed to the beast's spirit, asking that it give its life to benefit others.

MAIZE BLANKET

This woven wool Navajo blanket shows the sacred maize plant, and has a rainbow spirit surrounding it. Some American Indians believed maize had been given to them by gods called the 'Corn Mothers', and attached great importance to the crop. The Hopi Indians put a maize corn dolly, representing a Corn Mother, in a baby's bed for the first 20 days of its life.

Food & Drink

American Indian women were among the first people in the world to grow plants for food, and many of the foodstuffs eaten all over the world today comes from plants first domesticated in North America (including tomatoes, potatoes and maize). The introduction of the horse by Europeans made hunting the buffalo so easy that it changed the American Indian way of life. There was less need to cultivate crops, so agriculture regressed in some areas, and tribes became dependent on the buffalo. This made it easier for the Europeans to eventually defeat them (see pages 28–29).

HARVEST-TIME

American Indians viewed farming as women's work, although children and the elderly also took part. Apache Indians of the southwest planted small plots of land in the spring. A particularly lucky woman planted the seeds (unlucky women were never allowed to help), then tribes left their crops, living as hunter-gatherers until harvest-time. In autumn, when the song of the crickets changed, the Apaches knew it was time to harvest, and they returned to their farm and brought in the crops.

BUFFALO HUNT

By the 19th century, the buffalo hunt was at the centre of Plains Indians' life. It was the only time when strict discipline was enforced, since one wrong move could frighten away the herd. Hunting was the job of the warriors. The women and old men would drive the buffaloes towards the young men, who would kill them using bows and arrows or, later, guns. The young warriors regarded it as a great honour to provide meat for the children and old people.

FISHING

What American Indians ate depended on where they lived. The tribespeople of California were expert fishermen, but they also killed bear. In the Rocky Mountains, the Shoshoni ate antelope and rabbits, while in the Arctic, the Inuit hunted seals and whales. In the northeast, American Indians fished, and hunted moose and caribou.

RESPECT FOR NATURE

The American Indians ate a great variety of foods, but they believed that they were part of nature and treated it with respect. They celebrated nature and made dining bowls in the form of animals. The Shoshoni did not kill female animals during the breeding season, and some tribes would also pray to the plant spirits as they were harvested, and would apologize if they stood on an animal by accident.

BUFFALO

The buffalo supplied most of the wants of the Plains tribes. The tastiest cuts were eaten immediately in a great feast. The liver, tongue and soft nose gristle were eaten raw. The knuckle-bones were chewed as we would chew gum. The rest of the meat was dried, then pounded to powder and mixed with fat to make pemmican (a small cake made of shredded meat). The hide was used for clothing, bedding, bags (see left), shields, saddles, canoes and tepees. The hair and the sinews were used for bowstrings, rope and thread. The horns and bones were used for arrowheads, knives, tools, dice and cups. The hooves were used to make glue, the tail as a brush or a fly-swat, the tongue as a hairbrush and the fat to make soap.

Pastimes

The American Indians did not have 'leisure activities' in the way that we do today, purely for enjoyment. As well as being enjoyable, their games had clear functions within their society – such as to learn important skills, to woo spirits or to govern relations between the tribes. American Indians marked many occasions with ceremonial dances, but some also loved to race horses, gamble, play aggressive ball games with other tribes and perform simple rhythmic music.

PLAYING DICE

American Indians loved to gamble. They believed that success in a game of chance would give them long life, wealth, children or even good health. For the poorer members of the tribe, it was an accepted way of improving their status. Games included playing dice, playing *chungke* (a game which involved trying to throw wooden sticks into the centre of a disc) and *jacksnaps* (where counters are shaken in a basket; the player with the most counters left facing upwards wins).

RATTLE AND ROLL

While the American Indians of the northeast played flutes, many tribes did not have instruments that could carry a tune. Instead, they accompanied their dances with drum beats, rattles and chanting.

PLAYING LACROSSE

American Indians invented the game of lacrosse – although it was so rough that they called it 'little brother of war'. Tribes would sometimes play a ball game instead of going to war with each other. Teams comprised up to 100 players, and crowds of thousands would watch (and bet) on the result. The towns in the Creek Confederacy of tribes in the southeast chose their alliances based on the outcome of ball games; a town defeated four times in a row by a rival town joined its side.

MANDAN BUFFALO DANCE

Dancing was a way of communicating with the spirits. These Mandan dancers were trying to persuade the spirits to send buffalo for the hunt; their dance always worked, because it went on, day and night, until the buffalo appeared, however long it took. Dancing was central to the American Indian way of life. Some tribes had 'Eagle Dancers', whose swirling dance echoed the flight of the eagle, in a dance which brought peace. When it was trying to destroy American Indian culture in the 1880s, the US Bureau of Indian Affairs outlawed many dance ceremonies.

HORSE RACING

Many American Indian games were designed to improve hunting and fighting skills. Here, a group of Sioux warriors are taking part in a horse race. A similar game, intended to improve their horse-riding skills, involved galloping at full pace, then sliding down the side of the horse and firing arrows underneath the neck of the horse. In another game, braves would fire arrows into the air in quick succession, competing to see who could get the most into the air at once.

Fashion

CHIEF KEOKUK

Keokuk was the Chief of the Sauk Indians of the northeast. In this 1834 painting by George Catlin, Keokuk is shown astride his horse, wearing battle dress and a necklace of grizzly bear claws – an emblem of real heroism. He has shaved his head, apart from a long forelock, which he has threaded through the roach headdress to attach it to his scalp. The markings on his horse were meant to bring him success in battle. In fact, despite his warlike appearance, Keokuk always advised peace. In the end, he was poisoned by his own men, who betrayed him to government agents.

During ceremonial occasions such as potlatches, many American Indians wore clothes that had deep symbolical and religious meanings. At other times, clothes were designed to demonstrate the wearer's wealth or social standing. However, there is no doubt that the American Indians thoroughly enjoyed dressing up! A warrior would wear not only tribally-produced clothing, but also items he had acquired by trade – including blankets, European suits and even bowler hats.

SIOUX MOCCASINS

Sioux Indians of the Plains made moccasins from two pieces of buffalo hide (a sole and an upper) that were sewn together. The Blackfoot Indians of the Plains fashioned the moccasins out of a single piece of leather, which they folded upwards and sewed along the top. The shapes and colours of the beadwork were designed to bring the wearer into harmony with his environment.

SIOUX DEERSKIN DRESS

This dress was for public or ceremonial occasions. Dresses like these were made from two deerskins – one for the front, one for the back, with an extra piece used for the yoke. In typical Sioux style, it has long fringes and tassles, and the yoke is beautifully decorated with beads. The dress was designed to show off the wealth of the family and the skill of the dressmaker, and contained symbolism that related to the individual or their family.

ARAPAHO WAR BONNET

This is a typical Plains Indians' war bonnet. It is made from eagle feathers, tipped with horsehair and attached to a leather skull-cap. The bonnet is decorated with beadwork, red tradecloth and fur tassles. It would be worn only on important ceremonial occasions.

BEAR-CLAW NECKLACE

This picture shows a bear-claw necklace, such as that worn by Keokuk. American Indians wore many different kinds of jewellery, including necklaces, bracelets, rings, sashes, chokers, medals, bandoliers, armbands and breastplates. They painted their faces and bodies, and many of them were tattooed – the Pima Indians of the southwest believed that tattoos prevented wrinkles in old age.

ZUNI WOMAN

This Zuni woman from the southwest is wearing a homespun woollen *manta* over a cotton blouse. American Indians made use of the materials that were commonly found in their environment. Sioux Indians used buffalo or deerskins, but the Paiute Indians of the southwest used rabbit-skins and the Coos Indians of the northwest dressed their children in grasses and shredded bark. Archaeologists have even found one blanket made of 600 mouseskins.

NATIVE AMERICAN BEADWORK SADDLEBAG

Originally, American Indian women used porcupine quills for decoration, but they started to use beads after their introduction by the Europeans. American Indian beadwork is exceptionally skillful and beautiful, as the designs on this leather saddlebag show. All the designs have a ritual symbolism.

Art & Architecture

When Europeans saw how relaxed American Indians were, they accused them of being lazy. In fact, American Indians just had different priorities to the Europeans. Their way of life was extremely rigorous, but they made sure they left time for a rich cultural life. They loved arts and crafts, and used handcrafting techniques to produce lovely carvings, basketwork, beadwork and clothing (see pages 12–13). However, although much of what they made was very beautiful, it nearly always had a practical use.

PLAINS TEPEE

The Plains Indians did not build houses, they lived in tepees, which perfectly suited their nomadic way of life. They tied together poles to make a framework, and the covering, which required the skins of up to 14 buffaloes, was thrown over the framework and pegged to the ground. A hole at the top allowed smoke to escape. The American Indians covered the skins with drawings and designs, showing symbols of spiritual power they had seen in dreams or visions. The Plains Indians considered tepees the best place in the world to live. They were warm in winter, cool in summer and were easy to move. Tepee bases also formed the shape of a circle, which was the way in which it was believed the 'Power of the world' worked (see page 26).

ZUNI POTTERY

The Plains Indians did not make pottery – it would have been far too heavy to carry around as they moved from place to place. The Pueblo Indians, however, who lived in fixed settlements, became excellent potters. They formed a flat circular base of clay, then built up the shape of the pot by layering lengths of rolled clay and smoothing the surface using a wetted shell. This Zuni Indian carries a pot on her head. It is decorated with typical tri-coloured geometric designs.

PUEBLO INDIAN CLIFF PALACE

The Pueblo Indians lived in the dry, semi-desert canyons of the southwestern region. They built complicated tenements out of adobe clay bricks – the biggest apartment-blocks in America until the 19th century! Pueblo houses took full advantage of solar heating. In winter, when the sun was at an angle, the adobe walls absorbed the heat, and the retained heat kept the houses warm well into the night. In summer, when the sun was overhead, its rays fell on the flat, wood roofs, which reflected the heat and kept the houses cool.

GOING ON A BEAR HUNT

American Indian art was symbolic. When American Indian artists painted actual events, they used simple abstract drawings called pictographs, such as in this drawing of a bear hunt. They were not attempts to represent reality, but visual memory aids to remind the narrator of the details of the story. Europeans held a low opinion of American Indian art, and tried to get native children to draw 'properly'.

SIOUX HAND DRUM

The symbolic design on this drum shows a medicine man wearing a headdress of buffalo horns. It was designed to create a spiritual link between the animal and the people who depended on it.

Health & Medicine

CROW MEDICINE MAN

A medicine man, such as this Crow medicine man from the Plains did much more than just heal diseases. He was the person who enlisted the support of the spirits to help the tribe, knew the drum rhythms which would attract the spirits, could lead the hunters to food and sent magic arrows over the mountains to harm the tribe's enemies. He also gave general advice on everything from money matters to marital problems. Medicine men often became wealthy, because American Indians believed that the more you paid, the harder the medicine man would try to help you.

American Indians believed that the best way to keep healthy was to live a good life in harmony with Nature – disease came when that harmony was broken. Where illness did not have an obvious cause, it was believed it may have been caused by the magic of an enemy, by a ghost or because the patient had broken a tribal custom. The Cherokee Indians believed that disease came from the spirits of animals, who sought revenge for being hunted and killed. American Indian medicine men were highly skilled at using herbal medicines and, until the middle of the 19th century, were at least as effective as European doctors. They would not have continued to hold the respect of the tribe if their cures had not worked. However, their medicine could not cure European diseases such as smallpox, and whole communities were decimated with the arrival of these virulent new illnesses.

ROCKY MOUNTAIN IRIS

The American Indians knew thousands of herbal and plant cures. Scientists have found that many of them contain medicinal chemicals. For example, a medicine man would use white willow bark to cure a headache; today we know that it contains one of the ingredients in aspirin. The leaves of the Rocky Mountain Iris (shown in this picture) can heal septic cuts and ulcers and remove freckles. The roots, boiled and taken in small quantities, can be used to clean out and stimulate the digestive system.

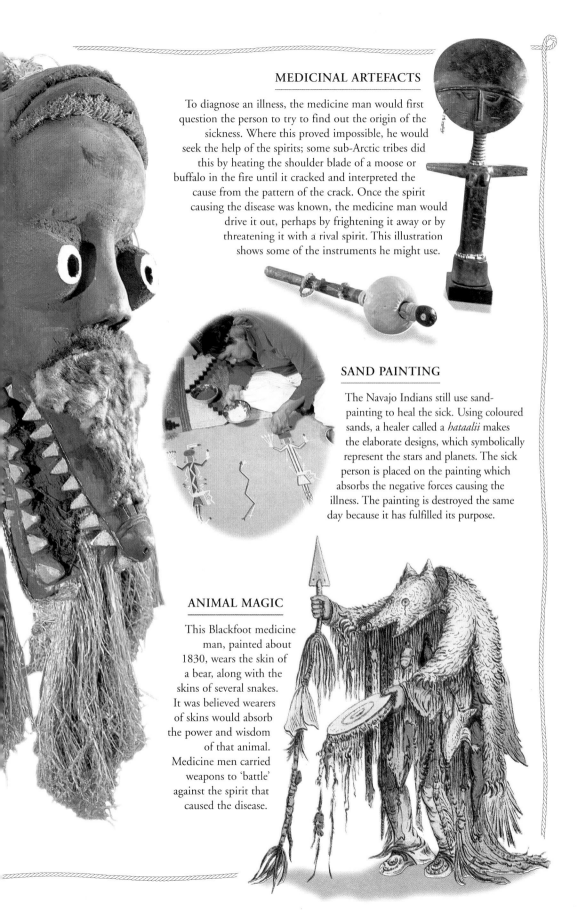

MEDICINAL ARTEFACTS

To diagnose an illness, the medicine man would first question the person to try to find out the origin of the sickness. Where this proved impossible, he would seek the help of the spirits; some sub-Arctic tribes did this by heating the shoulder blade of a moose or buffalo in the fire until it cracked and interpreted the cause from the pattern of the crack. Once the spirit causing the disease was known, the medicine man would drive it out, perhaps by frightening it away or by threatening it with a rival spirit. This illustration shows some of the instruments he might use.

SAND PAINTING

The Navajo Indians still use sand-painting to heal the sick. Using coloured sands, a healer called a *hataalii* makes the elaborate designs, which symbolically represent the stars and planets. The sick person is placed on the painting which absorbs the negative forces causing the illness. The painting is destroyed the same day because it has fulfilled its purpose.

ANIMAL MAGIC

This Blackfoot medicine man, painted about 1830, wears the skin of a bear, along with the skins of several snakes. It was believed wearers of skins would absorb the power and wisdom of that animal. Medicine men carried weapons to 'battle' against the spirit that caused the disease.

KWAKIUTL MARRIAGE

Here, a newly married couple from
the northwest sail back to the groom's
village. Among the Kwakiutl
Indians, a marriage was a way of
handing down the family property
to the daughter. If a man did not
have a daughter, sometimes he
would hold a ceremony to
'marry' a part of his body
(for instance his hand,
or a foot) to a young
man – who would thus
inherit his possessions.

EAGLE OF DELIGHT

Hayne Hudjihini, known as 'Eagle of Delight', was the
favourite of the five wives of Shaumonekusse, a
northeastern Indian chief who visited Washington DC
in 1822. In most Indian tribes, especially those who
lived on the Plains, polygamy (literally 'many
wives') was common. In a harsh environment,
where many men died prematurely, it was a way
for the tribe to provide for all the women. It was
also a way for a man to show that he was rich
enough to look after many wives and children. The
US President, James Monroe, found Eagle of Delight
pleasant and innocent. Unfortunately, she caught
measles on the visit, and died soon afterwards.

SPINNING A STORY

Navajo women believed that they had
been taught to weave by a spirit called
Spider Woman, and they handed down
both the skills and tools from mother to
daughter. During the 19th century, whit
traders forced the weavers to use chemic
dyes and imported fibres, but, after 192
the Navajo weavers returned to using
vegetable dyes. Navajo women use symb
of lightning and sunbeams in their desig
today as they did in the past. The early
Navajo blankets were designed to be wo
so their bright colours and designs could
seen 'in motion'.

Love & Marriage

In American Indian society, women were responsible for the day-to-day running of the family – maintaining the tepee; planting crops and carrying out other agricultural work; collecting food and firewood; and making clothing and crafts. Occasionally, women would fight – a Crow Indian story tells how an old woman named Strikes Two drove away a party of Sioux warriors armed only with a root digger, but the men did not like to talk about it! The women also conducted trade – European traders were surprised when they found themselves doing business with women. Some historians have written that Native American women became very rich selling sex to the Europeans in exchange for casks of rum, and then selling the rum on to the American Indian men.

A DOWRY OF HORSES

In most tribes, sweethearts were allowed to meet; in others, this was forbidden, in which case the young man would have to declare his love by playing loudly on a flute. Although some marriages were arranged, most young couples married for love. When he became a warrior at about age 17, a young man would ask the girl's father for permission to marry his daughter. He would be told to provide a dowry of horses or buffalo skins. This was not a payment but a measure of how much he loved her.

AN AMERICAN INDIAN FAMILY

Family was important to the American Indians but, in many tribes, the community was equally important. Sometimes, Inuit couples would change partners, and divorce was easy. On the Plains, a Cheyenne Indian simply had to throw a stick onto the ground and say 'I throw her away'. Any man who picked up the stick could become the new husband. However, the woman could take everything with her – the tepee, the tools and utensils, the fishing grounds and the children.

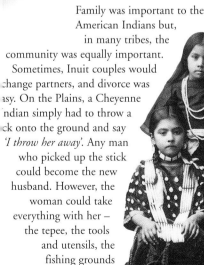

Children & Education

LEAVING HOME

At puberty, girls were able to marry and leave home, although Hopi girls had to first prove that they knew how to look after the household. Many American Indian tribes celebrated a girl's puberty with a ceremony or a feast. The Apache Indians covered the girl in yellow pollen; they believed that she was especially close to the spirits during this ceremony, and that she had the power to heal the sick by touching them.

American Indian parents rarely punished their children, and the worst that was done to them was to ignore their demands. Native children had a strict upbringing, and were required to grow up to be productive members of the tribe, but they were treated with love and kindness. The whole tribe helped to bring up the children – it was not just the parents' job. The Navajo word for aunt means 'little mother'. Children could wander into any tent and be looked after, and it was the responsibility of the tribe to take care of orphans. At age 10, many American Indian boys went to live with, and be trained by, their uncles. A Sioux proverb runs: *'Tell me and I will listen, show me and I will understand, involve me and I will learn'*, and it was by this principle that Sioux children were educated.

MEDICINE BUNDLE

Between the ages of 14 and 16, a boy would undergo an initiation to become a man. The Midewiwin Indians of the eastern woodlands held an initiation ceremony at which four or five medicine men shot the boys with hallucinogenic shells. In their ensuing dreams or hallucinations, the youths would 'see' a personal animal spirit friend, and were taught the secrets of adult life. When they came round, the youths would gather up a few items of religious significance to them, and keep them in a small pack called their 'medicine bundle'. This stayed with them for life.

LITTLE WARRIORS

Both male and female American Indian toddlers dressed up. This little boy is wearing the war bonnet of a great warrior. American Indian children were encouraged to speak out at tribal meetings. When a boy caught his first animal, even if it was just a rabbit, a feast was held to which even the chiefs were invited. Similarly, when a girl made her first beadwork tassle, her father wore it proudly.

SNAKE POUCH

When a baby was born in the Pima tribe, its face was painted with red ochre mixed with the mother's milk. The Pima believed that this would give the child good skin. The Sioux Indians kept the baby's umbilical cord in a specially-woven pouch. The pouch was hung from the baby's cradle in infancy, and carried by the child until puberty. The Sioux believed that this would keep the child safe.

ON THE MOVE

Carrying a baby in a backpack left both hands free for work. Over the baby's head is a projecting hood. When the mother stopped, she could lean the cradleboard against a tree knowing that, even if it fell over face-down, the baby's head would be protected. Many American Indian mothers hung coloured beads and trinkets from this hood to keep the baby amused as they walked.

EARLY LEARNING

American Indian girls loved to copy their mothers, and they would look after a puppy or a doll in the same way that their mothers cared for the babies. In this way their learned the skills of motherhood.

Weapons & Warfare

*T*he American Indians did not wage war for the same reasons as the white man. They did not do it to gain land, for they believed that no man could own the land, fighting instead for resources. They did not fight in armies like Europeans, and they believed that their first duty was to preserve their culture, tribal beliefs and families. Although American Indians had fought each other for as long as Europeans had, battles were not as bloody before the arrival of the white man and their superior military technology.

VALIANT WARRIORS

An American Indian fought for personal glory. Among the Plains Indians in particular, whose way of life discouraged them from gathering possessions or wealth, it was the main way to secure respect and honour from the other members of the tribe. Feathers worn by a warrior were a visual declaration of his exploits in war. A single red spot on a feather, for instance, could indicate an enemy killed in battle. Similarly, a split feather could indicate a warrior who had been wounded many times.

COUP STICK

Because a warrior wanted honour more than anything else, he often did not kill his enemy. Much braver than killing was to ride up to a live enemy and to hit him on the chest with a stick. This was called a coup. A warrior who had 'counted coup' many times was greatly honoured. He was rewarded with feathers in his headdress, which could be used to display status to others.

PIPES OF PEACE

This is a calumet – a peace pipe. A person carrying a peace pipe was safe wherever he went, and, even in the middle of a fierce battle, the warriors would stop fighting if it was held aloft.

SCALPING

Originally, only the Mohowk Indians of the northeast had taken scalps. As white settlers began to pay money for enemy Indian scalps (to prove that they had been killed), the practice spread to many tribes. The American Indians believed that, after death, their souls would go to the Happy Hunting Ground. There they would be pursued by their enemies – except those enemies who had been scalped. The soul of a scalped man became the possession of the victor.

INDIAN ATTACK

American Indians waged war in a very different way to Europeans. While European armies lined up and walked into the gunfire, Indian warriors would not attack technologically superior forces head on, preferring a swift ambush. To the white soldiers, however, this seemed like cowardice and treachery. Similarly, the greatest feat for an Indian warrior was to capture an enemy's horse, and war was the means by which most tribes obtained their horses. To the Europeans, however, horse-stealing was a crime punishable by hanging.

Transport & Technology

American Indians attitude towards technology was different to that of the Europeans. Where the white man tried to tame the earth and use it to make money, American Indians saw themselves as part of nature, and survived by adapting to and co-operating with it. The Europeans regarded the American Indians as savages, and they called the eastern tribes who adopted European technology 'the Civilized Tribes'. But in fact, American Indian ways were not inferior to European technology and were perfectly adapted to their own environment. Indeed, the first men to go eastwards into the American continent ('frontiersmen' such as Davy Crockett) wore buckskin clothes and adopted American Indian technology and skills.

SOAPSTONE PIPE

This pipe is carved from soapstone, which is soft and easy to fashion. American Indian technology was based around a series of skills – hunting, fishing, carpentry, weaving, sculpture – and their materials were all natural – skins, shells, feathers, wood and stone. It was 'craftwork' rather than technology in the modern sense.

LONGHOUSE WALL

Static tribes used available materials to build strong, comfortable homes. The Huron Indians of the northeast built large longhouses. They made a frame from saplings and covered it with bark and skins. Bark screens divided up the interior, so each family had its own living area. This photograph shows the wall of a longhouse; it is simple but effective technology. Huron longhouses were cool in summer, warm in the cold winters and strong enough to stand up to storms and heavy snow falls.

NORTHWESTERN CANOE

Canoes were built using local materials. The American Indians of the northwest made dug-out canoes like this one from the trunks of huge trees. Craftsmen dampened the wood and used hot stones to create steam to shape the sides. On the bows were painted pictures of moiety spirits – for instance, the killer whale, lord of the oceans.

GUNS

Through trade, American Indians managed to get many of the white man's utensils such as blankets, beads, kettles, metal knives, axes and especially guns. They not only used them to make life easier, but they thought these goods had religious and magical properties – a kettle that sang was seen as being alive, and a gun which roared and killed was a *manitou* (a supernatural spirit). The Algonquian Indians of the northeast bankrupted themselves, giving everything they had to get European trade goods to put in the graves of their dead.

SMOKE SIGNALS

American Indians had their own unique way of communication over long distances, as reliable as any European telegraph system. Messages were sent over great distances using smoke signals.

Religion

This is an eagle pole from an Indian burial place. The American Indians saw the eagle as a symbol of the power of the earth – it was graceful and beautiful, all-seeing, swift, powerful and vicious. Most American Indian tribes buried their dead in the open, on raised wooden platforms; they believed that, as the flesh rotted, the soul was released.

The first Europeans to visit North America decided that the American Indians had no religion, only superstition. In fact, the American Indians had a very sophisticated religion, which was inextricably woven into their everyday life. They prayed often, and held ceremonial dances before undertaking expeditions. They divided the year into a series of Thanksgiving ceremonies, to thank the spirits for their help. American Indian religion honoured the land, and they believed that *'all life is holy – the two-legged sharing it with the four-legged and the wings of the air, and all green things.'*

SNOW-SHOE DANCE

American Indians believed that the 'Great Spirit' created the world and that the 'Power of the world' worked in circles. The earth was round like a ball. The wind whirled round. Birds made their nests in circles. The seasons went round, and the life of humans was like a circle *'from childhood to childhood'.* In the same way, these Mandan dancers are moving round in a circle.

KACHINA DOLL

The Hopi Indians believed in spirits called *kachinas,* as they still do today. There are about 300 kachinas in all, although the Hopi have 30 *mong,* or chief kachinas. These spirits come from the underworld, and at one time used to live among the people, bringing them rain and good crops. But the people became disrespectful, so the kachinas left them. Now, they return during the six-month farming season, and each year kachina dancers dress up and impersonate them in a series of ceremonies.

TAMANAWIS

Instead of a Christian God, the American Indians believed that the world contained a complex web of 'powers' (or 'spirits') that affected life, for better or for worse. The American Indians of the northwest coast believed in *tamanawis* – spirit-familiars in half-human, half-animal form, who could help or harm an individual, and they made masks of these spirits.

SUN DANCE CEREMONY

Among most American Indian tribes, the main ceremony of the year was, and still is, the 'Sun Dance'. At the height of the ceremony, young warriors pushed skewers through their chest, and hung from them, until the flesh tore and they fell back. The Mandan Indians used the Sun Dance as a warrior's initiation ceremony – it was a way for a youth to show his courage and, through the pain, to see a vision of his 'spirit-friend'.

MOUNTAIN SPIRIT DANCE

In this dance, Apache Indians called 'devil dancers' dressed up as spirits. By doing so, they absorbed the powers of the spirits, and brought the tribe safety and success. Many dances were performed by 'secret societies' – the American Indians believed that secrecy gave their ritual dances more power. The dance is still performed today by the tribe.

SITTING BULL

In 1868, realizing the inevitable, the Sioux agreed to move onto a large reservation in the Black Hills of Dakota. But in 1874, gold was discovered there and prospectors flooded into the area. The American government sent in the army to take the goldfields by force. The Indians fought back, led by Sitting Bull, shown here, but were defeated. In 1889, the government took still more land from the Sioux. They tried to arrest Sitting Bull, but when his family protested, the police shot him dead.

Conflict with the White Man

The coming of the white man brought disaster for the American Indians. Although the American Indians won many battles, their victories provoked campaigns of mass slaughter. The American Indians were either killed or were forced to live as farmers on reservations. The Sioux chief Luther Standing Bear summed up their struggles with the white man: *'Only to the white man was Nature "a wilderness", and only to him was the land "infested" with "wild"' animals and "savage" people. To us it was tame. Not until the hairy man from the east came and with brutal frenzy heaped injustices upon our people did the "Wild West" begin for us.'*

BUFFALO SKULLS

The white men wanted the American Indians' land, so they took it. In the end, they decided that extermination was the best policy. US Army generals realized that on the Plains, the best way to wipe out the American Indians was to wipe out the buffalo on which they depended. *'Kill, skin and sell until the buffaloes are exterminated,'* said General Sheridan, *'then your prairies can be covered by cattle, cowboys and an advanced civilization'.*

CAPTURED BY INDIANS

'Save the last bullet for yourself', was the advice given to white men attacked by American Indians. However, although many American Indians scalped their victims, there were very few proven examples where Indians had purposely tortured their defeated enemies.

LITTLE BIGHORN

'Custer's Last Stand' has gone into history as the last battle of a hero against overwhelming odds. In fact, Custer was a fool who led his 200 men into a trap. The Little Bighorn was an American Indian victory, but it was also the start of their ultimate defeat. The US army responded with a series of winter campaigns, driving the Indians from their encampments (and their food reserves). In this way, they starved the Sioux into surrender.

GHOST DANCE

Life on the reservations was hard. Many Sioux warriors began a 'ghost dance' to persuade the Great Spirit to restore the old way of things. The dancers wore ghost shirts, which they believed would protect them from the white man's bullets. Just after Christmas 1890, the army arrested a group of about 350 ghost dancers, and took them to a place called Wounded Knee. There they shot dead some 180 men, women and children. This was the last attempt at American Indian resistance.

Legacy of the Past

TRADITIONAL COSTUME

Many American Indians dress up in traditional costume on ceremonial occasions. As well as keeping a link with the past, this is also seen as a way to communicate their differences intelligibly to white Americans. This girl is attending the Red Earth Festival, one of the largest American Indian meetings.

*U*ntil the middle of the last century, the American Government waged war on American Indian culture. In the 1940s, however, it introduced a compulsory programme which sent American Indian children to boarding schools where they were not allowed to speak their native language and were taught only English-American ways. Many American Indians were damaged by the ensuing loss of identity, and the tribes still have problems with alcoholism, drug abuse and disaffection. In 1944, however, the National Congress of American Indians was formed to re-assert the American Indians' identity. Nowadays, the American Indians form a vibrant, prosperous and assertive community. As a modern American Indian poet writes: *'I will not allow you to ignore me. 'I am living'. I am here.'*

EAGLE DANCER

One way that American Indians celebrate their culture is by holding large meetings called 'powwows', in which they meet together to re-enact the old dances and sing traditional songs.

DIRECT ACTION

Some American Indians are not satisfied just to celebrate native identity. They hold mass rallies and political protest meetings. In 1969, a group of activists took over Alcatraz, and in 1973, some American Indians occupied the church at Wounded Knee. By protesting, they are trying to get the US government to put right the wrongs of the past.

NAVAJO FAMILY

American Indian tribes nowadays make money from tourism. The problem with this, however, is that tourism forces American Indians to act how white Americans expect them to act. They are expected to be colourful, mystical 'children of nature', at peace with the environment. However, the money that tourism brings in helps aid new initiatives for native communities.

THE NAVAJO NATION

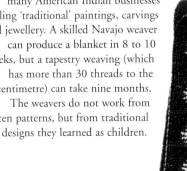

Since the 1960s, the US government has allowed the American Indians to run federal funding programmes for their own tribal members and also to run casinos. With the money they have received, the tribes have set up businesses and health and education programmes. Many American Indians today campaign for 'sovereignty' – the right to govern themselves within the USA. In doing this, however, the American Indians have had to act like American businessmen and politicians. Today, many American Indians want to 'build back', and to reinstate traditional tribal structures of government.

NAVAJO WEAVERS

In 1935 the Indian Arts and Crafts Board was set up to encourage traditional American Indian crafts. Today, there are many American Indian businesses selling 'traditional' paintings, carvings and jewellery. A skilled Navajo weaver can produce a blanket in 8 to 10 weeks, but a tapestry weaving (which has more than 30 threads to the centimetre) can take nine months. The weavers do not work from written patterns, but from traditional designs they learned as children.

DID YOU KNOW?

That in 1821, a Cherokee Indian named Sequoyah invented a phonetic alphabet of 86 characters? This allowed him to write down the Cherokee language. By 1825, most Cherokees were literate and, in 1828, the Cherokees started publishing *The Cherokee Phoenix*, the first American Indian newspaper.

That some deities were female? The Huron Indians believed the spirit-god who created the world was female. The Hurons' battle-cry was 'Wiiiii'; they believed that they had been taught it by a spirit-giant.

That some Indians were forbidden to speak in court? The state of Georgia passed a law in 1828 which forbade Indians to speak in court, even in their own self-defence.

That some tribes wanted to be sent to hell? When missionaries told the Huron Indians that, if they did not become Christians, they would go to hell, many Hurons said that they wanted to go to hell; they could not bear to go to heaven and leave their ancestors alone in such a terrible place.

That one white man was made an Indian Chief? In the 1830s, a remarkable English missionary named William Duncan settled amongst the Tsimshian Indians of the northwest. He started a Christian co-operative community, and eventually became the Chief.

That some tribes were suspicious of Christianity? When a missionary tried to convert the Iroquois Indians of the northeast to Christianity, he was told *'You have been preaching to the white people. We will wait a little while. If we find it makes them honest, and less disposed to cheat Indians, we will think about what you have said.'*

That violence could be a way to gain social status? Among the Tlingit Indians of the northwest, if you could not get social status by inheritance or marriage, it was regarded as quite acceptable to get it by murder!

That white Americans believed that American Indians treated their wives as 'slaves'? When the husband of a Chippewa Indian of the northeast died, she had to carry a large 'mourning bundle' for a year, during which time she could not remarry.

ACKNOWLEDGEMENTS

We would like to thank: John D. Clare, David Hobbs and Elizabeth Wiggans for their assistance.

Copyright © 2000 ticktock Publishing Ltd.

First published in Great Britain by ticktock Publishing Ltd., The Offices in the Square, Hadlow, Tonbridge, Kent, TN11 0DD. All rights reserved.

No part of this publication may be reproduced, stored in a retrieval system, or transmitted in any form or by any means electronic, mechanical, photocopying, recording or otherwise, without prior written permission of the copyright owner.

A CIP catalogue record for this book is available from the British Library. ISBN 1 86007 160 0 (paperback). ISBN 1 86007 227 5 (hardback).

Picture research by Image Select. Printed in Spain.

Picture Credits:
t=top, b=bottom, c=centre, l=left, r=right, OFC=outside front cover, IFC=inside front cover, IBC=inside back cover, OBC=outside back cover

AKG (London); 4tl, 5bl, 6/7m, 16tl, 19br, 22tl, 25t, 24/25m, 26b, 27b, 28tl. Ancient Art & Architecture; 2b, 3bl, 10bl, 27t. Ann Ronan/Image Select; 2tl. Art Resource; 6tl, 12t/l,14cr. e.t.archive; IFC, 3br, 8/9t, 11t, 17b. Corbis; 29b. Gamma; 12bl, 30/31c. Hulton Getty; 5tr, 6/7t, 18/19, 21t, 28/29b. Image Select; 14br. National Geographic; 18tl. Oxford Scientific; 16bl. Photri; 7cr. SIPA Press/Rex Pictures; 30b. Spectrum; 18bl, 30t. Still Pictures; 24tl.Superstock; 3c, 4/5c, 5cr, 8bl, 10/11c, 11b, 13r, 13bl, 14b, 16/17c & 17tr, 17c, 19tr, 20tl, 21br, 22/23 main, 27cl, 28b, 29t, 31t, 31b. Werner Forman; 8tl, 9cr, 12c, 14tl, 15b, 15t, 20bl, 20/21c, 21bl, 22bl, 23tl, 23tr, 24b, 26tl.

Every effort has been made to trace the copyright holders and we apologize in advance for any unintentional omissions.
We would be pleased to insert the appropriate acknowledgement in any subsequent edition of this publication.

DROUGHT
AND
PEOPLE

NIKKI BUNDEY

A ZOË BOOK

A ZOË BOOK

© 2001 Zoë Books Limited

Devised and produced by
Zoë Books Limited
15 Worthy Lane
Winchester
Hampshire SO23 7AB
England

First published in Great Britain in 2001 by
Zoë Books Limited
15 Worthy Lane
Winchester
Hampshire SO23 7AB

A record of the CIP data is available from the British
Library.

ISBN 1 86173 033 0

Printed in Italy by Grafedit SpA
Editor: Kath Davies
Design: Sterling Associates
Cover design: Ledgard Jepson
Illustrations: Artistic License/Tracy Fennell,
   Genny Haines
Production: Grahame Griffiths

Photographic acknowledgments
The publishers wish to acknowledge, with thanks,
the following photographic sources:

5b / Bibliothèque de l'Assemblée nationale, Paris /
9b / John Fox Images; Val & Alan Wilkinson - title
page / Philip Wolmuth 16 / 11t, 23t / Hutchison
Picture Library; Piers Cavendish 4,11b / Ben
Edwards 5t / Yann Arthus Bertrand 7 / Marco
Siqueira 8 / Caroline Penn 9t / Roger Scruton 13 /
Paul Forster 18t / Eliza Armstrong 18b / Javed A
Jafferji 19 / Material World 26 / Clive Shirley 28b /
Impact Photos; Jorgen Schytte - cover (inset) left,
24b / S Asad - cover (inset) right / Mark Edwards
10, 12b, 28t / Lior Rubin 17b / Adrian Arbib 22 /
Kevin Schafer 24t / Thomas Raupach 25 / DERA
27b / Edward Parker 29 / Still Pictures; M Jenkin
6t / J Sweeney 6b / H Rogers 12t, 27t / J Greenberg
14 / Eric Smith 15 / M Beard 17t / M Jellife 20t / B
Turner 20b / D Clegg 23b / TRIP.

The publishers have made every effort to trace the
copyright holders, but if they have inadvertently
overlooked any, they will be pleased to make the
necessary arrangement at the first opportunity.

CONTENTS

No clouds in the sky   4

Getting warm   6

Give me water!   8

Sun and skin   10

Dressing cool   12

Homes in hot lands   14

Farming in the heat   16

Sun-dried foods   18

Lonely lands   20

Desert expedition   22

Sun power   24

Forecasting drought   26

Fuelling the heat   28

Words we use   30

Index   32

All the words that appear in **bold** type are explained in Words we use on page 30.

NO CLOUDS IN THE SKY

All living things on Earth need warmth, light and water to stay alive. Without the Sun there would be no plants for food, no animals and no people. In hot weather, the Sun heats up **liquid** water in oceans, lakes and streams. Some of the water dries up or **evaporates**. It turns into a **gas** and hangs in the air. The gas is called **water vapour**. The more water vapour there is in the air, the hotter and damper we feel. Hot days can also be stuffy and **overcast**.

There are no clouds in the sky, so there will be no rain today. We love warmth and sunshine if we can keep cool and not get too thirsty. When it is too hot and dry, we are uncomfortable.

Droughts can happen in many parts of the world. They are most common in hot, **tropical** countries such as India. Without rain, plants droop and die and animals go thirsty. People become desperate for water.

We call unusually hot weather a **heat wave**. If there is no rain for a long time, we say this is a **drought**. The two often go together, but not always. The weather can also be cold and dry, or hot and rainy.

Long heat waves and droughts make life hard. People, plants and animals may even die.

Long ago, people believed that if the rains did not come, the gods must be angry. Tlaloc was the rain god of ancient Mexico. People danced and made sacrifices to him in times of drought. Today we know why droughts come, but we still cannot stop them from taking place.

5

GETTING WARM

Heat is measured as a **temperature**. There are different **scales**, such as Celsius (C) and Fahrenheit (F). The units of measurement are called **degrees** (°).

Humans are **warm-blooded** creatures. Our brains have **nerve cells** which can control the heat of our bodies. Unlike snakes or lizards, we do not rely on the Sun to stay warm.

The human body works best when the temperature inside the body is about 37°C. If the cells lose control, we suffer from **heat stroke**. If the body temperature rises above 42° or 43°C, we may die.

These instruments record the weather in a desert in the USA. We record temperature with instruments called **thermometers**. Warm air temperatures are normally between 15° and 30°C.

This tourist has collapsed on the beach, on a hot day. The brain cells which control her body temperature cannot cope with the heat. The best treatment for heat stroke is to cool the body as quickly as possible.

People with pale skins become red in the face when their bodies overheat. The colour is caused by the blood vessels which widen to let out body warmth.

Luckily, our bodies can lose heat in several ways. The heart pumps warm blood around our body through **blood vessels**. If the body overheats, the brain cells tell the vessels near the surface of the body to widen. Heat then passes out through tiny holes in the skin.

GIVE ME WATER!

Humans need water to stay alive. In many parts of the world, drinking water comes directly from a well, a river or a lake. The food we eat also contains water.

There is water in our blood, and our bodies use water for **digesting** food and for getting rid of poisons and waste. An adult human body normally contains about 20 litres of water.

On a hot day, we want to cool down. Cool water can lower our temperature and wash away stickiness, so we feel fresh.

In the desert, water is often a matter of life or death. We cannot survive for more than two or three days without taking in liquid.

The brain controls our temperature and also checks how much water our body contains. If we lose one-twentieth of the total our body contains, we feel thirsty. That is our body's way of telling us to drink water. If we lose one-fifth of the total, we risk our lives.

Water leaves our bodies in **sweat** and **urine**. In very hot, dry conditions we lose more water than usual.

Sweat helps to keep our bodies cool. It is like a sprinkler in a building or on a garden. Sweat makes our skin, and the air around it, cool and moist.

9

SUN AND SKIN

The Sun gives out a huge amount of **energy**. Energy reaches the Earth as heat, light or other kinds of **radiation**. One type of **ray** is called ultraviolet. Too much of this radiation causes sunburn on our skin. Sunbathing can dry out the skin and, over many years, cause serious illness.

We put special cream called sun block on our face or body on sunny days. It protects our skin from the ultraviolet radiation. Always wear sun block during sunny weather.

This girl from Nigeria, in Africa, has lots of melanin in her skin. It protects her against the Sun. People of African descent who live in cold countries still keep a dark skin colour.

When people with pale skin lie in the Sun, their skin produces extra melanin as a protection. The skin turns brown and tanned.

If we look at human skin under a **microscope**, we can see that skin has different layers. The top layer contains a natural colouring called **melanin**. This protects us from the Sun's rays. People whose families originally came from hot, sunny lands have a lot of melanin. It makes their skin brown or black.

DRESSING COOL

We wear shorts and T-shirts when the weather is hot. These clothes let heat escape easily from our bodies. We can wear long sleeves and hats to protect ourselves from sunburn or heat stroke.

This child has a sunshade, or parasol, fitted to her pushchair. It gives her shade and protects her from the heat.

Light colours, such as white, bounce back or reflect the rays of the Sun. Dark colours take in or absorb the warmth of the Sun.

The Tuareg people live in the Sahara Desert in North Africa. Their long, loose robes allow air to flow around the body, keeping it cool. Their heads are protected from heat and dust with long cloths.

Wind is usually cooling, so in hot countries, people may carry their own fans. They wave them to make a breeze. During a heat wave, we need shade. We can make our own shade by wearing a broad-brimmed hat. This stops the Sun from dazzling our eyes. Sun-glasses make it easier for us to see in bright sunlight.

People often wear hats and carry umbrellas in hot lands such as Malaysia.

HOMES IN HOT LANDS

In tropical countries, houses are designed to stay cool. They may have electric fans or **air conditioning**. For shade, there are shutters and blinds on the windows, or long porches and wide **eaves**. People plant shady trees around the houses and along the streets.

In many countries water is scarce. Every drop of precious rainwater is collected in pools or in tanks called cisterns.

A porch provides a barrier from the Sun's rays, and is open to any cooling breezes.

In Coober Pedy, Australia, opal miners have built underground houses. The houses stay cool when it is very hot outside.

Hot, dry weather affects many of the materials that we use to build houses. Metal swells, or **expands**, in the heat. It carries, or conducts, heat well, so a tin roof can become very hot. Paint dries out, cracks and peels. Tar and **asphalt** may melt.

Many insects live in tropical countries, and some of these, such as termites and ants, can destroy the timber used in houses.

See for Yourself

- Place pieces of wood, brick, glass, plastic and metal outside in the hot sunshine.
- After a few hours, which pieces feel the warmest?
- Which do you think are the best conductors of heat?
- Which would make the best building materials in hot lands?

FARMING IN THE HEAT

No crops could grow without the warmth and light of the Sun. Plants contain a green substance called **chlorophyll**. This works with sunlight to make the food which keeps plants alive.

Warm sunshine makes seeds start to grow, or germinate. It ripens fruit on the trees and grains of wheat in the fields.

Plants need water as well as heat. Hot countries with a high **rainfall** can produce tropical crops such as bananas.

Drought killed these crops in Zambia, Africa. Without water, crops droop or wilt and turn brown. Farmers have developed some grain crops which can survive in dry places.

In some hot, dry areas water comes to crops through pipes or channels. This is called **irrigation**. Irrigation makes it possible to farm even in the desert. Farmers in Israel use plastic to prevent moisture escaping from the soil as they grow crops in the desert.

Animals need water to drink, so a long drought may kill a farmer's cattle. Farmers may have to dig wells to reach water deep underground. Farmers fear very hot, dry weather. It can cause bush fires, or turn the soil into worthless dust.

See for Yourself

- Plant two trays with the same kind of seeds.
- Place one tray indoors on a warm, sunny window ledge.
- Put the other tray indoors in a cool, shady place.
- Water both trays equally.
- Which batch of seeds germinates first?

SUN-DRIED FOODS

Hot weather can make food go bad. Bread dries out and goes stale. Milk turns sour and tomatoes rot and become squashy. The food is spoiled by small living organisms called **bacteria**. Cold stops bacteria from spreading, which is why we use refrigerators to keep food fresh.

Bacteria have made these tomatoes go rotten. They are no longer safe to eat. They would have stayed fresh for longer in a cold place.

In many parts of India, people lay out fish in the Sun to dry out. Dried fish will not go bad, even in the hottest weather. They can be carried away easily to sell in other places.

Sun-drying preserves foods and also toasts or ripens them. These cloves are drying in the hot sun in Zanzibar.

Some foods are specially dried in warm air or in sunshine. Bacteria cannot grow in these foods, so they are **preserved**. We can eat some of these foods dry. We have to soak other foods with water before we can eat them.

Dried foods such as raisins, and apricots are on sale in most supermarkets. Sun-dried tomatoes come from Italy, dried mushrooms from China, and dried fish and meats from many parts of Asia and Africa.

See for Yourself

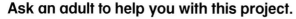

Ask an adult to help you with this project.
Some dried foods can be eaten only after they are soaked or cooked in water.

- Measure two cups of dry rice.

- Pour one cup of rice into a pan of boiling water and let it cook.

- Does the cooked rice take up more space than the dry rice?

- Is the cooked rice softer than the dry rice?
- Which kind of rice would you rather eat?

LONELY LANDS

Many people live in hot, wet places. Very few live in the world's dry regions, or arid zones. There is hardly any drinking water here and it is too dry to grow crops or raise cattle. Travel is difficult across soft sand or the baking rocks of a desert.

Some **nomads** and traders cross African and Asian deserts with their herds of goats and camels. They camp in tents. They travel from one watering place, or **oasis**, to another.

Nomads travel with their camels through the dry lands of northeast Africa. When the nomads stop to camp, they put up dome-shaped shelters covered in mats to protect them from the hot sun.

A nomad feeds his camel in the desert. There are no trees to shade them from the hot sun.

The oases are fed by wells or underground **springs**. People can grow a few crops there, such as dates, melons and figs.

Camels have **adapted** to desert life. They can travel for long journeys without water. The fatty humps on their backs give them the energy to carry on. Their thick eyelashes keep out the sand.

In some places, water gathers underground. People dig wells to tap this water supply.

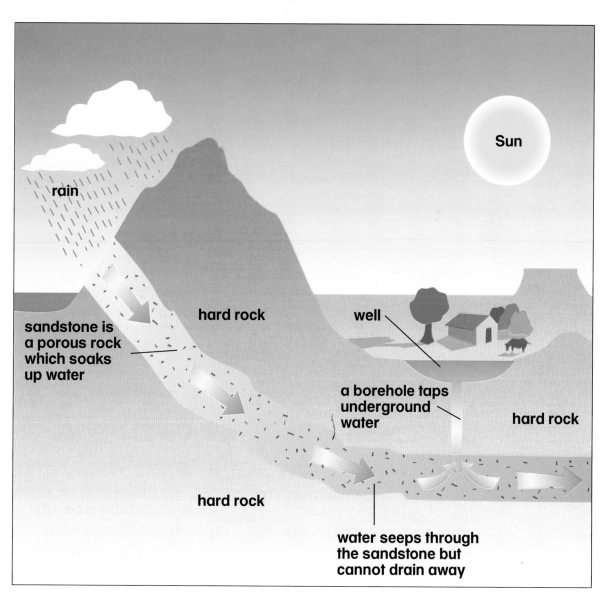

rain

Sun

hard rock

well

sandstone is a porous rock which soaks up water

a borehole taps underground water

hard rock

hard rock

water seeps through the sandstone but cannot drain away

DESERT EXPEDITION

Deserts are remote places, with few towns. People who go on desert expeditions must carry lots of water. Humans lose water rapidly in the heat. In arid conditions each person may need to drink between 10 and 25 litres of water a day.

Travellers use **compasses** to find the way. The compass needle always swings to the north. It is easy to get lost. In sandy deserts, the sand dunes shift with the wind. The shape of the landscape changes, and sand can bury road markers and signs.

Clothes protect the body against heat stroke and sunburn. But travellers need warm clothes too. Even in hot deserts nights can be bitterly cold. There are few clouds to trap the Earth's heat.

These sheep are suffering from a lack of water during a drought in Australia. The farmer uses a four-wheel drive vehicle as an ambulance. He will take the sheep to his farm where they can recover.

How would you drive across a hot desert? You would need a **four-wheel drive** vehicle to give extra grip, or **traction**. The tyres should be tough, to protect against thorns, but fairly smooth. Too much rubbing, or **friction**, disturbs the sand so that the wheels may sink in.

Truck drivers try to follow the tracks of other vehicles. Drivers lower the pressure of the tyres, so that they hug the ground.

Vehicles often get stuck in soft sand. The drivers have to dig the wheels free with spades. They push metal racks called ladders under each wheel, so that the tyre has something to grip.

SUN POWER

The Sun gives out power called **solar** energy. We collect this energy and use it here on Earth. A **solar panel** is a flat tile with a black surface, which absorbs the heat of the Sun. The glass on top helps to trap the heat in.

Solar panels can heat water or air. If tubes of water are surrounded by an airless space, or **vacuum**, they keep in their heat.

Solar **power stations** are used to produce electricity. The biggest one in the world is in California, USA. Huge mirrors point the Sun's rays on to a giant reflector.

Solar panels are often seen on roof tops in southern Europe as well as in Africa and Asia. The panels can power hot water and central heating systems.

Solar powered vehicles can travel at over 75kph. They do not give out fumes which **pollute**, or poison, the air. This car is travelling in Germany.

The vacuum stops heat escaping. It **insulates** the water, just as it does in the vacuum flasks we use to keep coffee warm. Solar power is a very **efficient** form of heating.

We use small **solar cells** made of **silicon** to turn sunlight into electricity. The cells can power calculators, vehicles or even spacecraft. Sun power can be used over and over again, unlike petrol or gas.

See for Yourself

- Fill a washing-up bowl with cool water and measure its temperature with a thermometer.

- Leave it out in hot sun for two hours. How many degrees hotter is it?

- Fill a vacuum flask with some of the water from the bowl. Leave the rest of the water in the bowl. Put the bowl and the flask in a cool, dark place indoors.

- After two hours, measure the temperature of the water in the bowl and in the flask.
- What is the difference between the two readings?

FORECASTING DROUGHT

All sorts of people need to know whether a heat wave or a drought is on the way. They may be farmers, water companies, builders, engineers or holiday makers.

Scientists called **meteorologists** prepare **weather forecasts**. They study the layer of air which surrounds our planet, the **atmosphere**. This presses down on the surface of the Earth. We measure **air pressure** with instruments called barometers.

These farmers are on their way to the market. They know that the weather forecast is for a very hot day. They travel at sunrise before it gets too hot. The cooler air helps keep their produce fresh.

Low pressure areas are called depressions. They bring warm, cloudy weather and showers of rain. High pressure areas are called anticyclones. They bring clear, sunny, dry weather, which may be hot or cold. Sometimes great **air masses** build up over land, and depressions cannot move in. These are the conditions that produce drought.

Water for cities and towns is stored in large pools or tanks called **reservoirs**. During droughts, reservoirs may run dry, which puts public health in danger. Water companies may have to limit the water supply. They ban the use of water in gardens or swimming pools.

Out in space, **satellites** whirl around the Earth. They track the movements of depressions and anticyclones.

FUELLING THE HEAT

When we use fuels such as petrol, oil and gas we pollute the Earth's atmosphere. Some of the fumes we pump into the air are made worse by sunlight. A thick **smog** can form. This makes it hard for people with an illness called **asthma** to breathe.

Gases form a layer in the atmosphere. It is like a blanket around the Earth. The gases trap heat around the Earth in the same way that a greenhouse traps warmth from the Sun.

Smog hangs over Djakarta, Indonesia. The pollution here was caused by forest fires over a vast area of Southeast Asia.

The number of people on Earth grows each year, and they all need food. But large areas of the world's farmland are turning into desert.

The Sun sets over Mexico City. Here the smog has been caused by pollution from traffic and factories. We depend on the Sun for our lives, but we must treat it with care.

This greenhouse effect is changing the world's **climate**. We call this change **global warming**. Deserts are spreading and ice is melting around the **Poles**. Other parts of the world are becoming stormier. Heat waves and droughts are becoming more common. If we reduce pollution we can make our planet a healthier – and cooler – place to live.

WORDS WE USE

adapt	To change to survive in particular conditions.
air conditioning	A machine which keeps the air in a room or a car cool.
air mass	A large, stable amount of air.
air pressure	The force with which the atmosphere presses down on a planet's surface.
asphalt	A black or dark brown substance, made from petroleum.
asthma	An illness which causes wheezing, coughing and difficulty in breathing.
atmosphere	The layer of gases surrounding a planet.
bacteria	Tiny living organisms, some of which can make us ill.
blood vessels	Tubes which carry blood around the body.
chlorophyll	A green substance, using sunlight to help plants make food.
climate	The pattern of weather in one place over a long period.
clove	A spice produced in tropical lands.
compass	An instrument used to find direction.
degree	A unit on a scale, such as those used to record temperatures.
digestion	The way the body absorbs what it needs from food.
drought	A long, dry period with little or no rainfall.
eaves	The edge of a roof, where it overhangs the building.
efficient	Doing the job well, with little waste.
energy	The power to make something move, or happen.
evaporate	To turn from liquid into gas.
expand	To take up more space, to swell.
four-wheel drive	A vehicle with four powered wheels, not just two.
friction	The force which slows one object down as it rubs against another.
gas	Any airy substance which fills the space in which it is contained.
global warming	The gradual heating up of our planet.
heat stroke	Collapse caused by over-heating of the body.
heat wave	An unusually long period of hot weather.
insulate	Using a cover to prevent heat loss or protect from electricity or sound.
irrigation	Bringing water to crops through pipes or channels.

liquid	A fluid substance, such as water.
melanin	A colouring or pigment found in human skin.
meteorologist	A scientist who studies weather conditions.
microscope	An instrument which makes very small objects look larger.
nerve cells	Cells which send signals between the brain and other parts of the body.
nomad	Some one who has no settled home, but moves from place to place.
oasis	A place where there is water in a desert.
overcast	Gloomy, blanketed in cloud.
Poles	The most northerly and southerly points of a planet.
pollute	To poison or make impure.
power station	A building or site where electricity is produced.
preserve	To keep fresh.
radiation	Giving out rays, such as heat or light.
rainfall	The amount of rain recorded in one place over a period.
ray	A beam of radiation, such as light.
reservoir	A lake or large tank used to store water.
satellite	A spacecraft which is sent up to circle a planet.
scale	A series of graded units.
silicon	Material found in the Earth's rocks, used in making computer chips.
smog	Fog mixed with smoke, or fumes from factories and traffic.
solar	To do with the Sun.
solar cell	A silicon chip which converts sunlight into electricity.
solar panel	A panel designed to make use of heat from the Sun.
spring	Underground streams of water.
sweat	Perspiration, moisture given out through the skin.
temperature	Warmth or coldness, measured in degrees.
thermometer	Any instrument used to measure temperature.
traction	The power to grip and move forward.
tropical	To do with the Tropics, the regions north and south of the Equator.
urine	Waste water passed from the body.
vacuum	An airless space.
warm-blooded	Having a warm, constant body temperature.
water vapour	An invisible gas, created when water evaporates.
weather forecast	An estimate or prediction about future weather conditions.

INDEX

air masses, 27
anticyclones, 27
asthma, 28

bacteria, 18, 19
blood, 7, 8
building materials, 15

camels, 20, 21
cattle, 17, 20
chlorophyll, 16
clothes, 12, 13, 22
compasses, 22
crops, 16, 17, 20

depressions, 27
deserts, 6, 9, 12, 17, 20, 22, 23, 28, 29
digestion, 8
dried foods, 18, 19
drought, 5, 17, 23, 26, 27, 29

energy, 10, 21, 24
evaporation, 4

fans, 13, 14
farming, 16, 17, 23, 26, 28
food, 4, 16, 18, 19, 28
friction, 23
fuel, 25, 28

gases, 4, 28
global warming, 29
greenhouse effect, 28, 29

heat stroke, 6, 12, 22
heat waves, 5, 13, 26, 29
houses, 14, 15

irrigation, 17

melanin, 11
meteorologists, 26

nomads, 20

oases, 20, 21

plants, 4, 5, 16
pollution, 25, 28, 29
preserved foods, 19

radiation, 10
rain, 4, 5, 14, 16, 27
rays, 10, 11, 12, 14
refrigeration, 18
reservoirs, 27

satellites, 27
seeds, 16, 17
shelter, 20
skin, 7, 9, 10, 11
smog, 28, 29
solar power, 24, 25
space, 27
Sun, 4, 10, 11, 12, 14, 16, 18, 20, 24, 25, 28, 29
sunburn, 10, 12, 22
sunshades, 12
sweat, 9

temperature, 6, 8, 9, 25
termites, 15
thermometers, 6, 25
traction, 23
tyres, 23

ultraviolet rays, 10

vacuum, 24, 25
vehicles, 23, 25, 29

water, 4, 8, 9, 14, 16, 17, 20, 21, 22, 23, 24, 27
water vapour, 4
weather forecasts, 26
wells, 8, 17, 21